Pen to Paper

Words Alive

Original title
Pen to Paper

Cover image
Moira Stevenson

Cover design
Sonja Smolec

Layout and edit
Sonja Smolec
Yossi Faybish

Published by
Aquillrelle

ISBN 978-1-4710-9393-7

Y000 842973

Foreword

Words Alive began as a taster course offered by Engage With Age in 2009 to encourage older people to meet together and try their hand at creative writing. The organisers had a theory. They knew that older folk are treasure houses when it comes to stories, and memories, having a lifetime of experience to draw on. They were aware that some of their members were keen readers and some already enjoyed being creative with the pen. They also knew that a lot of older folk do not get about easily and can feel isolated. So the class would be a way of testing the water, to see if there was an interest in meeting, sharing thoughts and recollections, and writing down what might otherwise be lost – in their own words, their own voices, with their own take on life. It would perhaps be a way of meeting several inter-connected needs and interests.

A year later, with the continued support of Engage With Age, a group emerged very keen to secure funding for a fully-fledged writing group for older people somewhere between 60 and 100 years of age. This was when Words Alive took on its name and proved Engage With Age right. The group includes first time and seasoned writers. It recognises the challenge of learning together when we have different requirements in order to hear and be heard, to understand and be understood.

I have had the good fortune to be the tutor/facilitator of *Words Alive* since its inception. Like everyone in the group I look forward to the two hours we spend in the library on Friday mornings, as they fill with stories and poems, company, creativity and craic. There is no doubt that individuals have gained confidence and encouragement from being in the group. Indeed, the group has been so productive that we have moved on to this next step of putting some of the work together into print and bringing it to a larger audience.

This collection of poems, stories, recollections and reflections gives us a slice of many lives and sensibilities. Some pieces evoke an era that seems light years from today, yet only yesterday. Others allow us to imagine what it might be like to stand in someone else's shoes – or bare feet! There is sadness, joy, anger, humour and insight. In the words of one of the members, Myra: "Please enjoy the writings of our group in this book and perhaps be inspired to put pen to paper yourself."

Ruth Carr

Acknowledgments

Words Alive gratefully acknowledges the financial assistance and support of Engage With Age and the Big Lottery Fund's Awards for All programme. The group would also like to thank Theresa McVeigh of Engage With Age, tutor Ruth Carr and volunteer Moira Stevenson for their expertise. Finally, a big thank you to John Galbraith, our Chairperson for his dedication, to John Galbraith junior for creating the *Words Alive* website and to Ballyhackamore Library and staff for giving the group houseroom.

Words Alive
http://www.wordsalive.webspace.virginmedia.com

Engage With Age,
36 Knockbreda Road, Belfast BT6 0JB
http://www.engagewithage.org.uk/

Big Lottery Fund's Awards for All programme
www.biglotteryfund.org.uk

Table of Contents

Jim Bradley

John Galbraith

Myra Gibson

Kate Glackin

Gladys Hull

David G Hull

Denis Hyde

Joan Lawlor

Jim McClean

Sue McCrory

John Mc Guckin

Marie Mathews

George Smythe

Diane Weiner

Margaret Wilson

In memory of our fellow writer and friend, Jim McClean

Jim Bradley

Message on a Bottle

A new day breaks with all its sounds: the birds singing their dawn choruses along with the pigeons cooing; the quiet noise of the early morning trolley bus; the busy blue bottle flying up and down, slipping and sliding as it buzzes and bumps against the slippery glass pane, trying to get through the glass. (Is it trying to escape from its enemies or find its breakfast?) The growls and barks of Patsy, our pet corgi, performing her security role when she hears the milkman coming. Because, be it sunshine, hail, rain or snow, along comes the clip-clop of the milkman's horse, as he pulls up outside our gate.

"Whoa, Bick," he says as he pulls on the reins.

Then the noise of his boots as they land on the flagged footpath, the rattle of pint milk bottles as he takes them out of the metal crate. Then the click of the brown wooden gate, his quick footstep as he walks up to the door, over the white gravel stones grinding and crushing them beneath his weight.

Reaching the front step, he sometimes hits the scraper with his boot. Clank clink you would hear, as he puts the new, fresh milk bottles down on the step and lifts the empty ones.

Back he goes with the empty bottles as they click into the crate pushing it over to the other empty ones with a bit of a crash. Then creaks and strains of the milk cart as he climbs back on, grabbing the reins, with a gentle flick of his wrist saying "gee up". The horse gives a shake of his head, a snort and a neigh as if to say OK, and off he goes, on to the next customer.

There's not so many milkmen today, but my thoughts go back to those days, as I look at my old, treasured pint milk bottle. It has lived in our kitchen for some time now. The name on this old milk bottle is *Agincourt Dairy, Jim Bradley, Castlereagh, Fresh Eggs daily.* It was one of my father's as he was the milkman I remember.

In The Garden

Scents of new mown grass,
Curry and lavender too,
Rosebuds wanting to spread.
Wintery weather still shows its face,
Summer is putting up a fight,
Showers and sunshine argue it out –
Seasons come and go.

The Irish Spring

April showers decided to come late,
Arriving in May with a temper.
Like a percussion orchestra
They tune up to entertain:
A few spits, a drop or two as they begin,
Then gentle drumbeats like a bird
Or a scampering animal
Pitter-pattering across the roof.
Then a cloud burst, bouncing heavy rain,
Puddles arrive out of nowhere.
Like hailstones these silvery grey notes
Do not miss their target,
Bless all living things with nourishment.

Autumn's Floor

Leaves gently falling
Floating down like feathers,
Some drifting in the cool, autumn breeze
Flickering down to rest with others.
Once green leaves that clothed,
Protected these deciduous trees,
Now heaped in small piles
Spread out across the land.
Moved around by the wind
Ending up floating on puddles,
Trying to enter through doors
Carried into homes on shoes
As people walk, children play,
Prancing and kicking them.
Sounds of rustling and squashing
As they travel on their way,
Leaving trees like skeletons so bare
Autumn mats and carpets,
Dying leaves of red and gold.

A Right Racket

As you walk up our drive,
Especially in the evening,
There is an area of bushes and small trees
With a few tall firs and even an apple tree
Standing between the drive and dual carriageway.
And every day you can hear a great debate –
Even above all the noise of diesel and petrol engines
And perhaps fire brigade, ambulance and police
With their sirens going nee-naw, nee-naw –
Little birds still chirp away among themselves.
It makes no difference to them what it's all about.
Do they have special meetings as they seem so busy?
Is one of them in charge of it all?
Are they chatting of their day's adventures,
Or maybe making plans of tomorrow?
More than likely they are booking their nests for the night.

Orange

For eating.
Its smell attracts me.
Even its skin
is good
for some conditions.

So many kinds
all with different skin
different sizes:
like people.

The orange at Christmas,
her favourite:
Terry's chocolate orange.
Talking about it
brings her back to me.

John Galbraith

The Street in Winter

Down the street a car draws away from the kerb,
it passes my window, slush spurts
from its tyres until it disappears.

The bedroom curtain across the street
moves slightly, a lit cigarette glows behind it.
A face appears at the window, then vanishes.

A man beats his arms against the snow,
he lifts his face to peer at the house numbers,
then staggers up the path across the way.

Raised voices stretch along the street
a door bangs off its hinges, then quiet
descends, each house seeking its own peace.

Templemore Avenue, Belfast 1942

A wet and windy afternoon in winter,
students bent over books in steady boredom
as slates are torn from the roof of their school.

The teacher an old man with a tired wrinkled face.
He rasps for order, from a throat
ruined by cheap cigarettes.

A black wig skitters about on his head.
Eyes closed, he waves his hands to a rhythm
that exists only in his mind.

More slates slip and we raise our heads
in horror as more planes thunder past.
Dust falls on our shoulders.

We begin our daily mantra:
ten times a hundred is a thousand
a thousand thousands is a million…

It's our maths lesson.

Searching for the Past

Looking for memories
in an old cardboard box
full of sepia photographs
I found my Grandad.

He stood beside my mother
his flat cap settled on his head
like a screwed top
on a Heinz sauce bottle.

His throat was scarred
by a celluloid collar
worn by working men
on a day at the seaside.

Mum wore a bathing suit
a lace hat hid her curls
they stood proud, paddling
on a summer's day at Millisle.

Washday

Grannie fits me
with a rubber apron
and wellie boots,
then hands over the wash plunger.

I slide carefully across the wet yard
to the big tub that holds Grandad's
boiler suits. My arms power the plunger
up and down like a steam pump piston.

Soapy water floods my boots,
Grannie lifts out a boiler-suit, places
it on the glass scrubbing board
that sits in the Belfast sink.

Suds fly, oil skims the surface,
then wet denim is placed in the mangle.
The rollers punish it until near dry.
Grannie pegs the boiler-suit onto the line.

One down, two more to follow.

First Love

They walked together, hand in hand,
she was drenched in cheap perfume,
he wore aftershave from Boots.

They stopped and he tasted scarlet lipstick.
Further down the road, progress halted
for a look into each other's eyes.

Wiser heads kept their distance.
Some smiled , recalled their own past.
First love, bursting, on a summer's day.

Morning with June

A summer morning,
the gentle light of dawn
sneaks past net curtains,
night begins to thaw.

June lies on her back,
gently snoring through open mouth.
Her mop of red hair spreads like a fan
over the white linen pillow.

A tiny drop of saliva
trembles in the corner of her mouth.
The alarm rattles, she opens her eyes
wipes her lips and snaps off the noise.

June lies back and yawns,
I place the breakfast tray beside her
and tell her that I love her,
because that's what dads are for.

Quick Response

The humid heat
is disturbed
by a monsoon rain
that has lost its way.
In the distance
a gong clangs,
traffic hugs
the curb.

A white van
with the word AMBULANCE
mirrored in red paint
on its bonnet
streaks up the road,
wheels spewing
out thin mud. The siren
howls like a hungry wolf.

Someone's in trouble.

Belfast Ink

He stands in his doorway
stripped to the waist,
tattoos showing the vanity
of a squandered youth.
What was once a declaration of power
still visible on his wrinkly skin.

An Indian dagger skewers
a heart that spurts blood.
A Chinese dragon has pounced
on his back. Another heart is etched
in jailhouse biro ink, it states
he loves his mum, forever and ever.

Now they are only coloured bruises
on the canvas of his worn-out body.
He is an old man long past his prime,
still standing in his doorway
stripped to the waist, dreaming.
Wasting the time he has left.

Winners and Losers

They stand outside the bookies,
gentlemen of leisure, working
out which horse will fly
first past the post in the next race.
A cheer rises from inside,
rollups are snatched from lips
and cast to the ground, as the punters
race to the door with betting slips
grasped in sweaty hands.
Soon the losers of the last race slouch
out and look around for a loan.
Winners saunter out laughing
heading for the pub.

Gone Shopping

Wasted legs in grey jogger pants,
sterile soled trainers with velcro straps
holding white bony feet.

He sits in a portable chair that's not a chair,
more a type of wheelbarrow
for an old man past his prime.

His son pushes him through the crowds,
the word "sorry" forever on their lips because
the wheelchair wheels nip at people's ankles.

The son takes out a tissue, stops pushing,
bends over and wipes his father's lips.
The old man looks up and nods.

He whispers thanks in a voice
ruined by eighty years of rough living.
They smile, and the sun comes out.

The Wheelie Shopper

The old man in his wheelchair
splattered with heavy rain,
wearing a shabby coat and greasy cap,
pushes himself through the shoppers.

His hands are worn and scarred,
pitted with blue black veins,
dirty and wrinkled like a miner's,
after a day down in darkness.

He strikes the wheels with his palms,
beats the rubber like a boxer.
When the chair slows, he lifts his fists
then pummels the wheels once again.

His face screws in concentration
as he safely drives the chair forward.
Slow, then fast, as it moves
to the rhythm in the old man's head.

It's Hell to be Old

It's Hell to be Old
Sitting here in my empty flat
My wife's gone and our bed's cold.

Everyone has left the fold
There's no mail on my mat
It's hell to be old.

My life's on hold
Haven't even got a cat
My wife's gone and our bed's cold.

Woman next door thinks I'm bold
All I wanted was a chat
It's hell to be old.

Can't drive anymore, the car's sold
Keep getting drunk, I'm turning to fat
My wife's gone and our bed's cold.

No-one left that I can scold
Family say I'll never make a diplomat
It's hell to be old
My wife's gone and our bed's cold.

Myra Gibson

Somewhere in France

This flower in a poem, for you

Somewhere in France a hero lies
Unknown in dust under the skies.
No more the sun need shine for him,
No more the sound of battle's din
Can wake him from death's finale.
Distant sounds of a reveille
Pass silent o'er his mound.

Somewhere in France your battle's done,
Back home the weeping long begun,
Weeping for one we know not where
To leave a flower or say a prayer.
No family footsteps tread your mound
Forever lost in earth's deep ground
Until the trumpet calls.

Somewhere in France a flower grows
Above your fragments in repose.
It blooms amidst death and decay
To permeate a summer day,
Its bright red petals glowing on.
Somewhere in France, constant and strong,
I leave this rose for you.

A nostalgic wander
through the Ulster Folk Museum, Cultra

There is a town in County Down born from planners' dreams
It never stood in bygone years yet has many scenes
Put together like a jigsaw each scene fits in place
To create a silent town that time cannot erase.
People's houses, people's shops even people's churches
Replanted in new earth that remembers and nurtures
An Ulster past that will not be forgotten.

As I wander through its streets into shops and houses
I find a strange emotion that in my eyes arouses
Visions of the people who once lived and worked here
The atmosphere of past life pervades and draws me near.
I can see the children playing hopscotch in the street
A horse in the blacksmith's forge waits for new horseshoe feet
While all around me kind voices wish me good day.

In the weaver's shed a lady sits beside her loom
A living weaver, had all my spirits gone too soon?
Still there's a dusty presence here not of her, nor me
Had all the spirits of weavers come along to see?
Her deft fingers working so skilfully at the loom
Then she stopped and the approving hosts were gone, too soon
And off I went to visit another room.
In the bank manager's home would there be intrusions?

Would the thought of his name diminish my illusions?
Yet there in his kitchen by his range stood my mother!
Getting ready to bake soda bread for our supper.
Be prepared when you visit this abiding small town
For the spirits of its past to follow you around.
It's time to go home, mother's coming with me.

A Woman Washing her Hair

I was reminded of our hair washing nights when I saw William Connor's pencil drawing of a woman washing her hair.

In our small kitchen house my mother washed and dried her son's short hair very quickly. I was the only daughter and I had long hair which took a long time to wash and dry. My head was plunged into a large basin of warm water taken from a sizzling hot pot on top of our imposing black range, then mother threw cupfuls of water over my head, then she used a bar of soap made frothy in her hands and put the froth all over my head. Her firm hands scrubbed soap into my hair with vigour, as if she were scrubbing her front doorstep.

When washed, I lifted my head out of the basin and waited until my mother got fresh water to rinse my hair, I can still see her running with the basin into the yard to throw the used water down the drain then return with a basin full of clean water taken from another pot of sizzling water from the range, cooled with water from the kitchen tap.

When my hair was rinsed I always looked forward to feeling the dry clean, plush towel being thrown over my head and mother rubbing my hair almost dry. I was always seated near the black range, the source of all the heat in the house. The range was kept working by opening a little door in the front of it and throwing shovels of coal inside it, this little door was opened very slightly to speed up the drying of my hair. Mother always reminded me to not sit too near the range "Don't get close, you could get burnt."

I cannot forget those long winter nights when sitting with damp hair was a miserable memory to me. Of course I can never forget the heat that came from the slight opening of the little door of the black range, the heat crept into our bones, warming our small kitchen house and throwing out a red glow that was reflected in all our faces. My mother's own loving and kindly face always outshone the glow from her cosy black range.

Years later when the range was carted down the street to make way for a modern open fireplace, I heard my mother say "I have lost a friend."

On the boardwalk at Atlantic City

On the boardwalk, not far from the vibrant sea,
Sat a man in a wheelchair.

My emotions disturbed, I hurried on,
Only to find another one, with his friend,
Both sitting at the end of the boardwalk,
Two more men in wheelchairs.

Were they buskers? Were they beggars?
I heard no singing, no begging with their voices.

They were asking this world to understand,
That once they were strong and healthy,
Young men full of life, like the vibrant sea,
They faced today, sitting in their wheelchairs.

And hoping for someone to pass their way,
And look with compassion at the words
                    A Veteran of Vietnam
Written by them on a sand-spattered piece of wood,
Blown in by the vibrant sea,
To rest in their wheelchairs.

Love dispersed

I saw her in the library
She wore a chiffon scarf
The colours of leaves in heaps.
It was Autumn when she left me pining
In sleepless sleep.

She passed me in the library
Without a glance, as her brown
Chiffon scarf fell to her feet
And all the leaves of Autumn smothered me
In sleepless heaps.

Haiku

I realise too late
My train was not on track
Love derailed for ever

Dream's Illusion

In dreams you spoke to me,
Your sound resounding
Into the sweetest music,
My soul in peace surrounding,
Yet my own heart was pounding
For you to come to me.

Your voice called out to me,
Its reverberations
Fading slowly in the night
With dream's anticipations.
I face this resignation,
I cannot go to you.

The Skylark

I envy this joyous singer
And his high flying in the air,
In those summer skies he lingers
Without sorrow, without a care.
A surging freedom moves his wings,
He revels in God's awesome sky
With opulent sounds, on he sings
Taking his voice to realms up high,
While I on earth must strive and plod
With my feet firmly on the ground,
My wingless shape no nearer God
My human voice restrained and bound.
In dreams I'll fly up in his sound
Heavenward soaring from this mound.

In Praise of Harvest

I lived in a house in a street in Belfast; there were no trees or flowers growing in the street. I was very young when my aunt took me to my first harvest service in our local church; I admired all the beautiful flowers, all the colours of the rainbow that surrounded me in the church.

There were plump green cabbages and creamy white cauliflowers arranged in rows up and down the hallway into the church. Random baskets of red and green shiny apples were placed round the choir stalls.

Sheaves of wheat, tied in bundles, straight from a farm sat sturdily at the back of the church, beautiful crisp brown harvest loaves were arranged neatly in large wicker baskets. At each end of that most special place, the communion table, stood grand, sleek, real silver vases filled with glorious flowers.

We sang many wonderful hymns, it is little wonder that the Harvest Service has become, for me, a beautiful, colourful contrast to the grassless, colourless street in which I lived.

Many years later I became a soloist and one of my most memorable engagements was in a little country church to sing at their Harvest Service. I sat in the choir stalls waiting to sing my solo "How lovely are thy dwellings." I looked at all the harvest splendour that was inspiration for my solo. I made my way up to the pulpit and while waiting for the organist to play my introduction my eyes fell on a harvest loaf in front of me, my eyes could not miss the small harvest mouse greedily gnawing his way into the loaf. All around me the choir members were squirming with horror at this defenceless little creature. I knew that the little mouse had every right to be there; somehow his presence completed the harvest scene for me. When I stopped singing the mouse was still eating, oblivious of me and the glorious harvest scene that he chose to become a part of. The choir's last hymn was:

> *All things bright and beautiful*
> *All creatures great and small*
> *All things wise and wonderful*
> *The Lord God made them all.*

Kate Glackin

The Shiny Blue Sequinned Jacket

Great excitement among my friends! "The Good Old Days" was being performed in the Grand Opera House, and Frankie Vaughan was the special guest. We had four weeks to beg, borrow or buy our Victorian costumes for the big event in the autumn of October 1986. We booked the two front rows and 20 of us prepared ourselves for this special evening – ten ladies and ten men – what excitement!

Most of my friends hired suitable outfits from Elliotts of Ann Street, but I decided my long black skirt and white cotton long-sleeved blouse with mandarin collar and lace cuffs would be most appropriate. I borrowed my mother's black-brimmed hat, decorated it with red and pink roses, and I felt great, except there was something missing when I admired myself in the mirror. My outfit needed a colourful jacket. Time was against me, and I began to panic. I asked all my friends, but nothing suitable came my way.

I was losing heart and became very despondent. On the Sunday morning before the show, my very best friend Trudi arrived at my door with a large parcel. She knew I needed a colourful jacket to compliment my outfit. Apparently her neighbour, aged 90, had died, and kindly bestowed to her this beautiful edge-to-edge, blue sequinned jacket. Trudi said it was much too small for her and I was very welcome to wear it to the Opera House and to keep it. I tried it on immediately. It was magnificent, perfect fit, sparkling blue, glamorous and it complemented the outfit. I knew I looked gorgeous, and felt ready for the big night.

We all met at the Opera House on the special night, admiring one another and looking forward to participating in the "old time" songs. I felt very proud and excited. I knew my outfit was the most stunning of them all, and I was aware I was the centre of attraction and the envy of other onlookers.

We settled into our seats at the front of the stage beside our husbands and waited patiently for Frankie Vaughan to appear. He looked so handsome, tall, lean and had dark, thick, curly hair. He sang his song "The Green Door" and we all participated and swooned. He requested one lady from the audience to come up to the stage and accompany him to sing "Give me the Moonlight". The lights were switched on and my jacket sparkled. He came down from the stage, took me by the hand, and brought me up to sing with him. I was shaking with joy and pride. I whispered to him "why did you choose me?" and he said "it was your magnificent jacket that dazzled me."

What a wonderful time we all shared, never to be forgotten. That night I gently folded my jacket between white tissue paper and pressed it into a large box. I loved it, it was so extra special.

Two days later, my friend Trudi arrived at my door looking rather worried. She said, "Kate, you know my little neighbour who died and left me the blue sequinned jacket? Well, her daughter came back from Canada to finalize the clearance of the house, and asked me did I know where the sparkling jacket was." I said I had it, and she asked me to return it to her as she had given it to her mother as a Christmas gift some years ago.

Trudi was very upset and totally embarrassed at having to give me this news. I was broken-hearted when I handed her the box with the jacket inside. However, I did put it on for the last time, put my hands in each pocket, and pulled out a ticket. It read "The Good Old Days" music hall evening at the Grand Opera House: special guest, Frankie Vaughan.

My memorable Blue Sequinned Jacket has gone forever, but to this day I still cherish that extra-special ticket to prove I was there!

The Soup Kitchen

That's what my mother called our kitchen on a Saturday night. At 7 o'clock we three sisters aged six, eight and ten were propped up on high stools with our little pinnies securely tied around our waists and our feet dangling under the long pine table. Mum would pull the large gingham plastic tablecloth out of the drawer and cover the table completely. We were each given a pair of blunt scissors, a bunch of parsley, celery and leeks, already washed, and the preparation of the soup began. Mum supervised every snip we made while she scraped and diced the carrots, parsnips and potatoes.

The big, black, shiny soup pot hung on a large hook over the black range, filled to the brim with hot water simmering the barley, lentils, peas and a two pound piece of shin and marrow bone. Mum wore a colourful turban around her fair, curly hair with a large bow at the front and we had our long hair neatly plaited and tied at the ends with blue, satin ribbons. Our tabby cat lay on the rag rug Mum had made from scraps of material left over from the dresses and coats she made for us on the Singer sewing machine at her Haslam class. Tigger kept purring contentedly, licking his coat and enjoying the heat of the range.

At 8 o'clock Dad pushed open the front door and whistled up the hall "You are my sunshine". He kissed

Mum and each of us in turn and fell into his favourite armchair. He filled his pipe with Erinmore tobacco and after a few puffs he fell asleep.

We whispered to one another, "Dad is exhausted; he must have had a busy day."

Mum smiled and said, "Tut, tut. It was the game of snooker and the pint of Guinness that knocked him off his feet!"

We chuckled, listening to the cat purring and Dad snoring. By this time our little chores were complete. All the vegetables were washed and scooped into the soup pot to gently bubble all night. We cleared the table, put the gingham cloth away and took off our pinnies, all in order for next week's soup night. Mum rewarded us with three cups of Ovaltine and three digestive biscuits. Dad awoke, lit up his pipe again and switched on the wireless and listened to "Dick Barton, special agent". Mum put the pan on and prepared Dad's favourite Saturday night fry.

We said our prayers on our knees and thanked God for all our blessings. Dad carried us up to bed and Mum followed with our hot water bottles, tucking us in and thanking us for helping her with the soup–making. We soon fell asleep with the comforting smells of the vegetable soup and Dad's tobacco.

It's time for me to make my weekly vegetable soup, now that winter is approaching. Alas, no Mum to supervise me, no Dad to smoke tobacco. They passed away many years ago, the tabby cat gone too. My two sisters married, live a distance away. I buy my mixed soup veg in a see-through packet, along with the carrots and parsnips. No marrow bone now, just soup mix from a tin. No black range to cook on, to comfort and keep us warm. All gone.

Oh how I miss the smell of the weekly, bubbling soup and Dad's Erinmore; all the innocent fun of our weekly soup kitchen.

Gladys Hull

Pony and Trap

Saint Stephen's Green
bathed in glorious sunshine,
Molly Malone still much alive.
Nellie stood out among the buzz,
dressed to kill,
brown and beige polished shoes
scraping the tarmac, she beckons to me.
Gently I stroke her
between two winking hazel eyes
and discover she's addicted
to my wine gums.
Drooling for more, tempting me
into the glossy, gleaming trap
of fifty euros a mile.
I just smiled and took her photo,
then settled for a coffee.
Myriad wildlife dined free
in the park that morning.
Bye Nellie, see you next time.

Bally Cultra

Scent of printer's ink
I can almost hear
The clatter of the press
And in the church
A solitude.
Mill workers, memories
My mother's labour of love
For a pittance.
Script in hand I stand
And gaze at empty drug jars.
The vacant doctor's chair –
Perhaps next year.

My Colour

Blue
The sea
Old U.T.A. buses
An azure summer coat
My budgie

Yet I'm never blue.

Remembering the Floral Hall

The Saturday night ball
One night stands
Lifelong romances too -
Till sports closed it down.
Return, my rendezvous!

A Busker I knew

Strums my favourite tune...
Dropping coins in his upturned hat
I recognize my school day pal.

Giving up

Sugar levels soar –
No more sweet treats!
Resigned to fruit and yoghurt.

Sea Shell

Solitary, sandy
Waiting for a rising tide
Sea gulls hovering.

My Great Uncle

Deep sea trials over,
The Pride of Belfast sailed.
Southampton bade adieu,
Cork beckoned, all is well –
Unsinkable!

Luxury liner westward bound
Blue ribbon record was in mind
Atlantic never seemed so tame
Safe in the hands of Captain Tom
Full throttle.

Icy mines would pose no threat
To the monster of the sea.
Crow's nest alert –
A greater monster looms!
Evasive action all too late
As watertight sections were sliced
As a knife through cheese.

The doom of fifteen hundred souls
Was sealed
Unthinkable!
Now sinking fast
Lifeboats alas too few,

As the band played on
My uncle Tom stood on the bridge
His retirement a watery grave.
Only his cap survived.
Titanic Quarter tells the rest,
Costly the lessons learned.

Gladys and David Hull

On a Sheep Farm in Moneymore

When first I heard it,
thought it a swear word.
My friend
– when in doubt
or something was against –
he simply said
fornenst.

Viewpoint

Panning for gold in the Sperrins
Five hundred feet above sea level
Panoramic view of five counties
Shared with ewes and suckling lambs.

Giant Jigsaw

Shoulder to shoulder
Boulder to Boulder
Slab to Slivers
Pyramid edifice
A-line shaped.
Teams made up from
Male & Female
Older & Younger
Disabled & Able –
A motley crew.
Builders
Without mortar, or plumb line,
Width gauge a simple twig,
No trowel or spirit level,
Basic tool-kit of spades,
Shovels, pickaxes, sledges,
On with protective gear.
Fine quarry dust
Slips through my fingers.
The work is steady
The craic is good.
Nature looks on –
Lowing cattle,
Buzzards hover overhead,
Little robins steal our crumbs

Creepy crawlies all round.
Foundation stones of body weight
Topped with jagged rocks:
Our dry stone wall
Must stand the test
As over our work of art
With hobnails boots he plods.
No movement!
Job well done!
This mended wall must last
Against the elements' icy blast
Two centuries from now.

A Dead Ringer

Best suit, butterfly collar and tie.
He lies serene in a coffin made of wood.
Heart of gold, not very old.
A long rope tied to his big toe.
Would the bell toll before interment?

Solitude

Like sunset on a silvery strand
a silhouette
darkness and light fused
blended hues
soft
gentle on the mind
sanctuary
for the man within
sublime
serene
sleepy shades of the same colour…

A Busker (I got to know)

Midnight deluge.
Magee Clock echoes
through deserted Bangor streets.

Huddled in the shadows
of a dim doorway,
no plectrum –
skinless fingertips
pluck well-tuned strings.

Songs of yesteryear
around my open fire
'til breakfast time.

Robben Island

Bathed against backdrop of blood, sweat and tears
Native tribes suppressed over many, many years
Out of Natal's womb arises a special boy
Whose vision for freedom sprang from inner joy.

All civil rights denied, homeland not home but hell,
Apartheid's poisonous power, all's not well.
Deprived of the staff of life, no vote just hate
As national, brutal forces plundered and raped.

Nelson Mandela led from behind the scenes
Uniting blacks, spearheading long lost dreams.
Afrikaners shaken right to the core
The bird with the broken wing was yet to soar.

Hunted and hounded by undercover cops
Finally the beagle, bleeding drops.
In chains and manacles seaward bound
Incarceration worse than an animal pound.

His youthful inner joy they sought to kill
Torture, starvation did not break his will.
Egg on many faces, long overdue –
For almost three decades they let Mandela stew.

Pardon at last, leader forth he came,
To break an iron yoke, tribute to his name.
From Robben Island to dignity and renown –
Hail, South Africa, liberty's golden dawn.

Denis Hyde

Pen to Paper

Write something –
out of ink.

Today the sky
is not out of blue.

The dog barks.
Someone at the door?

Nobody there.
My mind wanders…

Thoughts drip like ink
onto the page.

Here

Here in my bed, awakened by bacon frying –
coming through from the scullery.

Here my bedroom floor is cold to the touch –
feet on bare lino.

Here my mother put a bucket, filled with cold water,
adding Dreft and dirty clothes, on the top of the gas stove.
She lit it with the battery gas lighter and the blue flame popped up.
Maybe half an hour later, they are boiled clean.

Here the door knocked hard,
Margaret from across the road
with a plate of home made meringues
filled with gooey fresh cream
comes in for a chat and a cuppa.

Coffee Pot

I am brand new
shiny, bought from
a department store,
brought home and filled with
hot, hot water. Someone pours
some freshly ground
coffee inside me and
waits until I'm infused.
The room has suddenly
that wonderful fragrance
of freshly ground coffee.
I am ready to pour into
dainty cups. Do you take
your coffee black or white?
MMM D E E L I C I O U S !

The Old Days

Gas fire, gas fridge,
Our neighbour's electric clock,
TV rental and unsliced bread,
Swings on lamp posts in the street.

Fireplaces in attic rooms
Milk floats, Paris buns,
Sugar in blue bags,
Cow's udder and pig's feet.

A rag woman calling "Any oul' rags".
And men with carts of herring,
Wee Alfie the dwarf from Castlereagh
A man selling bleach on a bike each week.

The Ambassador, the Castle, the Picture Drome,
Blue bag for whites
And red Lifebuoy soap,
Five Boys choc bar and big jars of sweets.

The mangle in the yard.
The Nit Nurse in school,
Ciggie coupons to collect and
Rhubarb dipped in sugar for a treat.

Rainy Day Pennies

Remember rainy days
counting rainy day money
we saved up in a jar.
Brown and silver coins
putting them into money bags
taking them to the bank
getting them changed
to pounds and pence –
Father saying:
"Spend it wisely."

Mum Says

"Never wear green,
it's bad luck."
But I went shopping,
bought a blue and green shirt.
When I showed it to mum
she went daft.
All this fuss for nothing
Because I'm colour blind.

The Leaves

The wind is blowing hard
and the leaves are turning
red and gold.
They appear to be on fire.
I love to kick them,
it makes me feel
like a child again.

Harvest

Golden wheat in the field
waiting to be harvested.
Golden straws with the Sun
shining on them, just like
Necklaces, lost in the field.

Wounded

Helpless and weak
Shot by the enemy
Can't move
So painful
Shout for help
Wait a bit longer
Here come the boys
Glad to see them
Give me first aid on the field
Gunfire blasts from somewhere
Stretcher ready for me
Heard them say 'he is badly wounded'
Need to go to hospital
Bit bumpy on the truck
More blasts
Swerve to avoid the holes
Arrive safely
Nurses and doctors attend me right away
One of them says 'you are lucky to survive'
'You deserve a medal'.

Please Speak Clearly

Come closer to me
So that I can read your lips.
Please speak clearly, don't mumble
And please don't shout.
Forgive me if I ask you to repeat yourself,
I need to see you speak because I'm deaf.

Joan Lawlor

Things I am glad of...

- Glad that both of my parents lived into their eighties, with all their faculties; and at the end, as my dad would have said, "they got away easy".
- Glad that I live in my head. It's like having a twin brother who fits into my skin, down to the last finger and toe.
- Glad that we have running water.
- Glad of the past, when we had interesting friends who talked and laughed til two and three in the morning.
- Glad of nature's gifts: green fields, trees, flowers, rivers, sea, mountains. They enhance the quality of life.
- Glad when the night is dark and still and my dear friend the wind comes out and knocks my window, and if I'm lucky I get a special whistle.
- Glad when I meet people who think like me, only different.
- Glad when it stops raining and the sun comes out.
- Glad to have experienced the love of my daughter's dog who lived with her in Bangor and yet knew before Susan did, and cried every time, when the ambulance came to my house in Belfast.
- Glad to live in a country where we can go to school and learn to read and write and count our pennies or pounds.

A poem in the making

I lay in my bed all morning
Bleeding my mind,
The transfusion of time wasted.
Ill-fitting words dumped
Like malformed vessels,
Hurled off the potter's wheel.

Old Age

Old age is for others. When I hear of an old person's age, I think: I'm that age too, but no matter how long I live, I will never believe I am an old age pensioner. Others: yes; not me!

It's good to wake up in the morning. And if I do, I feel I will see the day out.

I like clothes and I often think of old people I knew as a child and the clothes they wore. I can't imagine any of them wearing my clothes.

I think there is no-one like myself and always have. Nowadays people are told to love themselves as a good therapy. So I was well before my time!

Jim McClean

Hard of Hearing

Jack was hard of hearing. That meant he could hear some sounds and could benefit from hearing aids. He wasn't totally deaf, or profoundly deaf, as they say in the trade. He was also a bit artistically challenged. So, with this combination, his decision to join a newly formed writers' group beggars belief. Probably something to do with a shy but talented friend who desired company.

Jack wasn't a very productive member of the group, so, no doubt with a degree of desperation, the tutor suggested he write something about his disability as he felt so strongly about it. Jack agreed and mentioned that he had already begun a poem along these lines.

Jack searched out his earlier effort which he had entitled H.O.H. That is, Hard of Hearing. It borrowed heavily from a leaflet he had picked up in a lip reading class. The first verse went thus:

"It doesn't matter."… "Never mind."
I don't think you meant to be unkind.
But said in response to, "Say that again",
Can cause a person like me hurt and some pain.

Warming to his task he dreamed up a second verse:

When chatting please speak up and slow your pace,
And it's very important we speak face to face.
Lip reading is difficult and tiring but hey!
If I can't see your face, I can't see what you say.

Jack's third verse continued the theme:

Please don't speak with your back to me or from another room,
And trying to chat in a noisy crowd is headed for certain doom.

By this stage Jack felt that he had flogged this aspect of deafness to death and should embark on another thing which he found irritating. Namely, situations in which those suffering from the disability were treated as figures of fun. This would often happen when a person who was hard of hearing joined a small group and, in the course of conversation, someone might tell a joke or story with a punch line or funny ending. On many occasions the afflicted will not hear the latter properly and whilst the others are doubled over with laughter, he or she is still waiting for the ending with maybe a blank expression, only to become the focus of continued laughter for their lack of humour, or for being slightly dim.

Jack attempted again and again to convert these feelings into verse but clearly the computer Poetry Wizard was having a day off, or maybe even a week.

Eventually he gave up and decided to move on to the final verse. He had another bone to pick in relation to how deaf people were treated, and this concerned the use of insulting descriptions applied to the victim. He himself had been described as "tinned beef". Words presumably used by the semi-literate to rhyme with their pronunciation of deaf as "deef". When attempting to convert this annoyance into verse, Jack again encountered a brick wall, so he decided to work on his closing lines which, surprisingly, had begun to form in his mind, albeit they needed some editing. Here he wanted to indicate to his reader the extent to which the problems of the hearing impaired were so grossly underrated.

A major problem with hearing loss is feeling isolated,
And as a serious disability it is seriously underrated.

Jack decided that, provided the writing group didn't excommunicate him, he would in future stick to prose and hoped that in due course he would learn how to write and appreciate poetry which didn't have to rhyme.

Staging Point

There was once a little village in what we now call East Belfast
Where the coachmen changed their steeds in days of yore,
Its name tells what went on there in the not so distant past,
Yes, we still know it as Ballyhackamore.

Sue McCrory

Squirrel Haiku

I watched the squirrel
eating his breakfast
as I ate mine.

I watched him chewing
discarding the chestnut shell
over the garden.

A frosty morning
and my squirrel doesn't come.
I waited and waited.

Little Bird

It was a long time ago when I first drew breath at my grandmother's home. My birth weight was two pounds, four and a half ounces.

The midwife said, "Too small, every day she will need twenty four hour attention."

My grandmother quickly replied, "I'll look after her."

I had no nails, nor eye lashes, no hair and my skin was very dry. Every day my grandmother rubbed olive oil into my body, taking care not to remove any skin.

She kept me alive by feeding me a small drop of milk through the filter of a fountain pen. Grandmother fed me this small portion of food several times daily.

She always kept me warm, she held me in her arms and had a special nursery chair that was just the right height to allow her to get up easily, we were a cosy pair.

My grandmother held me close to her heart, our two heartbeats united in the enjoyment of the healthy warm glow that came from the welcoming open fire.

It was hard work for her looking after me twentyfour hours every day. I know it was a labour of love, Some times her arms would grow weary from holding me all the time. She called me her "Little Bird" and put me in a shoe box fitted out with a layer of cosy and warm cotton wool. Off I would go to sleep.

My grandmother did all this for me during the first six months of my life, she did it without a break. She kept surrounding me with love and care, enabling me to soon become a healthy and contented baby.

THANK YOU GRANNY

You Are

You are
the robin redbreast in my garden.
You are
the rain that washes my boots.
You are
a star at night, so bright.
You are
the automatic door that opens for me.
You are
the tap that gives me water.
You are
the bush that gives me a white rose.

A Canny Shopper

When I returned my shopping trolley to its stand, I discovered a pound coin left in another trolley, I put it in my pocket and then left the store.

The next store I went to was a multi-store, it was offering bargains in a sale. I spied a cardboard box lying on the floor and opened it, inside was a pair of shoes.

I tried the shoes on to see if they were the right size for me. They were a perfect fit, and at a knockdown price of seven pounds and fifty pence. But there was a sticker on one of the soles stating that the shoes had been further reduced to five pounds.

I hastily went to the check out and set them on the counter, only to find I had only one pound and seventy pence in my bag. I told the assistant.

She asked, "Are you sure you have haven't enough money?"

When she saw that I was very distressed she checked her till again.

She told me, "There is a further reduction of three pounds."

I still hadn't got enough money to buy the shoes. Then I remembered the pound coin that I had taken from the trolley. I searched my pockets and put together an assortment of coins. I gave the assistant two pounds for a pair of shoes that originally cost seven pounds and fifty pence.

Thank you, my unknown benefactor. Your pound was put to a good cause and thank you to the shop assistant who was determined to sell me those shoes, no matter what the cost.

A Spontaneous Kindness

Another true story

It was a Saturday evening, I was on my way to visit a friend. I called into a store to get a few items. I took them to the check-out and then I realized I was twenty-seven pence short. There was a queue behind me, all adults, and not one I knew. What would I do?

Then a small hand reached over to me with coins in it. I looked round. The owner of the hand was a young boy who spoke to me.

"I don't need this change. I have already paid for my shopping. You can have it."

I thanked him and paid for my goods. I was overwhelmed by the young boy's kindness, a most welcome gesture to me amidst a shop full of adults.

John Mc Guckin

Dare to Dream

Don't daydream!
How often did I hear those words.
Sit up straight!
Stop looking out the window!
Why are you reading those comics?
You'll never amount to anything!

All designed to keep you in line.
Those of us who dare to dream, create -
perhaps words on a page, maybe a painting,
a sketch - all conceived from dreaming.
We dream, then create the reality.
Do not stop looking out that window.

Imagination leads to many places.
Follow your dreams,
don't let other people be your guide.
You and I are on the road where myth and magic
draw breath side by side.
Beyond the blinkered lines, imagine…
Dare to dream.

In my Life

Life and colour: yellow, mellow, fading sunlight
draws me forward. I'm a drifter, forever
moving on towards never ending roadways.
Never have I consciously thought out or through
the consequences of actions that came
to dominate my life:
Shall we marry? OK.
Shall we buy a house? OK .
Shall we have children? OK.
Shall we move house? OK .
Will you divorce me? OK .
Still on the impulsive tread-mill of moving on,
I look towards far distant horizons,
sunlight bathing them in yellow, mellow hue
and think, time I moved on…
Forever drifting in my life.

Yesterday's Man

Driving through a yesterday land
I chanced upon a yesterday man
gazing forlorn at his yesterday home.
Its cold, boarded-up look belied
the warmth in its yesterday hearth:
love and affection, stories and songs
lost to future despair.
Yesterday's country folk gone,
no more easy talk or slow moving carts,
just fast cars never slowing to spare
a thought for a yesterday man
gazing forlorn at his yesterday home.

Reason to Believe

I have reason to be thankful.

Why – because I have reason to believe in love.
Love is beyond reason, yet love does not discriminate:
it bestows grandeur on the poorest, majesty on the richest.
The illogical splendour of being in love is unreasonable,
yet I have reason to believe in love.

I have lived, I have loved, and in my family I find love still.
No need to look for love, it lives inside each of us.
Reach out, embrace the one you are with, you may find
you too, have reason to believe in love.

The music of love is silent, loud, raucous, and lost in mystery.
That moment, when you suddenly raise up your voice, and say
I LOVE YOU, and mean it, lets you know
that you have reason to believe.

Love is magnificence.
There is no other way in the world to live
than to be in love, and say I love you.
Try it, grasp the reason to believe.

Just thought of something. It's really, really important.

Now what was it? Oh I know, it was, it was…
Let's see, I went over there and, then I put
out my hand and then… I don't remember,
although, it seemed important when I went to do it.

OK. I'll start over, trace the proverbial steps
from here to there. Steps retraced, hand outstretched, and
nothing. Wrack the leaking brain, put the metaphorical
plugs in place. Now what have we got?

Ach, I don't know… It was something useful, I think.
What – just something I used to know. Now, although
it's important, my leaking brain refuses to acknowledge
me plugging the leaks. You'd think it had a mind of its own.

Right, John, sit down: you went over there, to do what?
I don't know. Just thought it was important, won't dwell on it.
Next time I think of something really, really important
I'll write it down – maybe…

Belfast Giants

Living in this city where
metal giants dominate our skyline,
their ribbons of steel rusting.
Where only ghosts of ships remain,
where Samson and Goliath
wait for Belfast to build real ships again.

Belfast once stood proud on giant shoulders
forged by its workers:
women of the mills, men of the shipyards,
factories supplying steel, linen, hemp, ships, aircraft.
Belfast once stood tall on workers' backs, but now
Tears of rust stream down these mighty, metal giants' flanks.

Life's lesson

I have lived a life of delicate lies
built on gossamer webs.
Tissue built
then destroyed.
Memories of schemes lost.

11/11/11

Out here on the choppy sea,
watching Dover recede
into the gentle mist of England,
all is not serene.

We sail towards a harbour,
one we have been told is as dark as Hades,
young men, comrades all,
aboard this troop ship.

We could not envisage the despair
that would make us weep
listening to the dying screams
of comrades all sacrificed.

Seventeen days of Hell.
How can a man withstand such grave insanity –
Ypres, Somme, Passchendaele, Lys,
And Flanders field left full.

We few left behind in Hades know
the red poppy blows gently for freedom
at the going down of the sun and at its rising.
And we remember them.

Marie Mathews

Where I started my School Days

At the little school in Tullyallen
A three mile walk there and back
The winding lanes devoid of cars,
Ponies and traps, and the lovely
Green fields and few people.

Passing through the graveyard,
No thought of death on your mind
As a four year old.
And still I visit there
Where the school is long since gone
And my grandparents lie buried
In the earth of Tullyallen.

My Life

I was born in the Royal Maternity Hospital on 10th April, 1936. I was brought up in a caring environment and spent a couple of my early years with my Grandparents in Drogheda, county Louth. I attended my first school there in Tullyallen. I remember the coal fire in the grate and the desks with little ink holders. My two brothers and I walked three miles to get to school and three miles back.

We then returned to Belfast and continued at a primary school there. Next I progressed to the Sacred Heart of Mary Convent School at Lisburn. It was difficult as you had to learn so many subjects and of course, manners were very important. We knew nothing of the facts of life as the nuns taught you nothing in that respect. In fact, when I look back, I realize that I was so innocent.

I left school and took up a position in the Civil Service. I remained there working in various departments until my retirement, 13 years ago. I had to leave for a couple of years prior to that to look after my elderly parents who both suffered strokes. However, I was able to resume employment for a few years.

I had a wonderful home life. We always had our meals sitting round a large, dining room table sharing our stories of the day. My late Mother was a good plain cook who made lovely food and I don't remember anything being left on our plates.

I have had my ups and downs, but I look back on a life full of lovely memories.

Remembering Pen and Ink

The watery blue ink that got everywhere,
That worked its way into my face.

The callous that formed on the skin of my middle finger
Because of the pressure of holding the dip pen.

You could even smell the ink as it dried
In the inkwell into a gritty blue residue.

Handwriting is deeply individual
As unique as the human face.

When you receive a handwritten letter
You can tell who it's from by the writing.

I always wrote to my two late aunts
One in Maidenhead, the other in Australia.

Grown deaf and out of touch with new ways
They loved getting letters to paint them a picture.

Recently I read that the state of Indiana
Has given up teaching handwriting.

The dip pen and ink confined to history
The watery blue ink replaced by computer keys.

Dating across the Divide

An aunt of mine, a lifetime ago as a young catholic girl, was walking out with a protestant boy. She always arranged to meet him at the Hippodrome and on numerous occasions she found that the back of her dress, cardigan or coat was quite wet. She could not understand this. Whenever she was getting dressed her clothes were perfectly dry. Her boyfriend remarked on the wetness.

"Why is your back always wet?"

It was only many years later, after the romance finished and her mother had died, that she discovered the cause. Each time she walked out the door to meet her boyfriend, her mother raised a vessel full of holy water and sprinkled it liberally on her back. Her mother must have thought she was going to meet the devil because he was a protestant and the holy water was to protect her beloved daughter.

How times have changed!

Haiku

My lovely hat
A Philip Tracey creation
A coif of ribbons.

Words Alive class
A meeting of great minds - alas
Shakespeare I'm not!

The tennis season
Grunts and groans abound – are they
Winners or losers?

My Mother

As a young girl my mother embarked on her secondary education with an order of nuns in Belgium. This was paid for by her aunts who were spinsters and in business. Her mother had been left a widow with 6 daughters at the age of 38, so their generous offer was much appreciated. My mother recounted many stories of her stay there until she was 21 when her sister, Claire asked her "Are you going to stay there forever!"

One of the many stories she told was about bath time. When taking a bath she had to keep her dressing gown on in the bath as the nuns did not want anyone looking at their own body! How you managed to wash properly beggars belief! The nuns would come in to make sure that you had your robe on throughout.

All the same, my mother loved her time there. She studied music. How times have changed. Now young women can walk the streets half naked if they like. But that was 91 years ago!

The Knock on the Door

On the 23 rd May, 1986 at approximately 12 pm several loud knocks broke the peace, followed by a long ring of the doorbell at our home, number 90, Botanic Avenue.

My mother rushed up the long hall to the front door. She was confronted by a police sergeant who asked for her by name. He said he had sad news for her. The New York Police Department had rung Donegall Pass R.U.C. station (that was the one nearest by). He asked had she a son called Raymond Mathews. When she replied yes he said,

"I have to tell you that he was found dead in bed in the George Washington Hotel, in Lexington Avenue, New York by one of the maids cleaning the room in the morning."

Of course, my mother was frantic and asked, "Are you sure it is him?" It was. They had found his passport in his room. My brother Raymond worked in the hotel business and lived in that hotel. He was unmarried and died at the age of forty-seven, the youngest of the three of us, a brilliant scholar but a dreadful smoker. He just ate them. On many occasions he fell asleep with one between his fingers. He would not stop, nor did he like you saying to him to stop. It was perhaps the pressure of his work. He was very thin but he had a massive heart attack. The arteries were all clogged.

At secondary school Raymond had always wanted to go to New York and this he did, leaving to work there at the age of 21. I had many, wonderful holidays in New York with him and stayed in beautiful hotels.

My brother Tony and I went over there to identify him as our mother was unable to travel due to illness. We rang her every night and she still did not believe her son was dead. He was buried there as he would have wished, after days spent going to the morgue, getting autopsy reports, putting up with the dreadful heat and the callousness of the funeral home. They just seemed to be interested in money.

So the New York I loved at one time took on a tragic side for us. My father had died four years earlier and my mother died six years later. I think she never got over it. I will never forget that knock on our door.

The Pawn-broker's

The first thing that strikes you of course, are the three golden balls. Apparently they date back to the 15th century when the Italian Medici family had a crest of 6 balls. There was a falling out between two families and they ended up with 3 balls each on their crest. Then one family entered into the business of money-lending and the 3 balls became associated with the business of the pawnbroker.

Pawn-broking became big business and highly successful in the bad old days of the early 1900s in my native Belfast. Poverty was rife and it was a means of existence for a lot of people. It was a sad episode in our history. You pawned your jewellery or your suit and the pawn-broker gave you what he thought was a fair price. You got a ticket and you could redeem it after a while, if you had the money. But if you didn't come back after a certain time (I think it was 3 months) they could sell it. I think the going rate for a gent's two-piece suit was £2 and three-piece suit, which was quite common in the 1950s was approximately £3. It was a business that made money and a very comfortable living at that for the three balls.

I remember a true story where a mother sent her young son equipped with a very large statue of the Virgin Mary to the pawnbroker. It was bigger than he was! He said, "I couldn't carry that!" So his mother wrapped it in newspaper and stuck it into a pram which was in their hall. When he got to the pawn shop, the pawn-broker undid the parcel and when he saw the statue he nearly had a heart attack. His shop was situated in a protestant area of the city. He said, "I don't want the statue but I will take the pram!"

I think that the younger generation thought that the pawn-broker's was a dry cleaner's. You put your suit in on a Monday and you got it out on a Friday. But thank God people are now better off and pawn-broking has virtually died out, except for C J Geddis on the Albertbridge Road. However, having said that, it has become big business in London because of the economic downturn. It is a means of getting money quickly as banks are not giving loans and requires no form filling. You leave in your prized possessions (a Picasso or a Van Gogh, perhaps) and you get cash over the counter.

The biggest pawn-brokers in Victoria, London are thriving. They take in anything worth a fortune – Rembrandts, Porsches, Ferraris – but they draw the line at airplanes as they can't store them and apparently they're not in demand. If you don't come back, they can sell the booty so they are well protected. So they are the only ones making a fortune today.

Perhaps in these hard times I could go into competition with Geddis, but I think it would upset me too much. On the other hand, I might …!

George Smythe

Lamp Posts for Goals

In our day – and actually seeing a picture of a Lamplighter brought it to my mind – we used to use the lamp post to play football. That was the goals and the lamp post on the other side was your opponent's. We used to be afraid of the police. We never would have attacked them at all. If we were playing football and we saw a policeman going down the Castlereagh Road or down Donovan Parade, we used to run. But the main part of my story is that in those days none of us had watches, or if we did, we didn't take them out when we were playing football. And my father used to say to me and my younger brother:

"Now be sure to come in when the lights go on."

But this night the lights didn't go on. We were out playing and when I got home I told my father the lights didn't go on. And he didn't believe me. So I got a caning. It wasn't a matter of "just go up to bed." I got caned. It wasn't my fault, but I had my younger brother with me you see, and I was to look after him.

Ravenscroft Primary School

I went to Ravenscroft Primary School and there I met my very best friend. His mother and my mother signed us in at the same time and he has been a best friend of mine for seventy years. We still keep in touch.

Now a lot of people in East Belfast will know who I'm talking about when I mention that it was George Lemon who used to have a fruiterer's shop, not very far from the Holywood Arches. Now in school, we were taught to knit while the girls were cooking. I remember them bringing in these big yellow bone needles with the black knobs on the end and the wool. Then the girls came round with what they'd baked and we got a sample of whatever it was and they made tea.

Looking at the photograph of Ravenscroft Avenue devastated during the Second World War blitz, it occurs to me that we never thought that the place would be bombed where we were playing a couple of weeks before. I firmly believe that they were trying to bomb the Arches or the railway and that was how the school got hit. Luckily, of course, we were off school when it happened.

Big enough for Boots

The only birthday I clearly recall
Was the year I was given boots.
My three younger brothers sulked in their gutties,
Envied my firstborn right to leather –
Not regular black, but brown, long-laced leather boots.
"Now George," my mother reminded,
"you've only to wear them out when it's wet!"
That night in bed I prayed for rain,
My brown boots side by side by the po,
Biding their time,
Toes tucked under my dreams.

Breathe in

Smell the roses
Do not pick them –
Leave them for another nose.

George Smythe remembers his days as a Chorister

I was one of the eight boys who were selected to sing at Lord Carson's funeral. Captain Brennan who was the City organist was also the organist in St Anne's Cathedral. Well he brought us all out to the steps at the front and we could see the cortege coming down Donegall Street with the Union Jack and all on it. And then we went into our choir stalls and Lord Carson was brought in to a crypt which was actually selected inside the cathedral. When he was carried in he was to be put in what we would call a tomb and Captain Brennan brought us down to the grave and we all stood round it.

Then we all sang, "As in Adam all die, even so in Christ shall all be made alive." We never thought anything about it because we had rehearsed it in the cathedral. But after a while when you get older, you come to realise that this actually came from the Messiah by Handel. And the words were like a poem. It's a thing that will stick in my memory all my life.

I later became a member of the past Choristers' Association and I was selected to sing in Canterbury Cathedral for the bicentennial celebrations. There were boys there from all over, Leicester, London and so forth. That was one of my experiences but all my life was musical and I was singing. For instance, Lord Cleaver was having a concert in the City Hall and I was to sing at it. So he sent his chauffeur out to collect me and when he came to our door, my mother had my younger brother in her arms and she thought that I'd put a pirrie through a window of somebody's big house. He asked "Is George in?" And of course, I'd told my mother there was a car coming to collect me, and then this Rolls Royce arrives up and out steps a chauffeur in his cap and uniform. So I got into the Rolls Royce and whenever you get into a car like that you fall back, so I couldn't see out the window. But I was waving to my mother and she was waving to me and we couldn't see each other.

The next day when I went to school, they were all asking, "Who was that came up to your house?" We were living in an ordinary semi in Blenheim Drive and, you know, you would never have got a Rolls Royce and a chauffeur there, let alone me getting into the car! But I was privileged to have sung for Lord Cleaver of Robinson & Cleaver. I was boy treble then and on the programme alongside the likes of John McCormick and also Anne Ziegler and Webster Booth. And I had that programme autographed, but in the upheaval of moving several times it has been lost.

I've been down to the Telegraph and they are trying to get me the back copy in which Carson's funeral was reported. I remember there were men sitting up on the big arms of the gas lamps in the street to see it all. It's a thing I'll never forget.

Our Firstborn – nearly 70 years ago!

I wanted to be with my wife when she gave birth to our first child. I'd been with her when the baby was conceived and it made sense to me to be with her when the baby would be born. At that time I was training to be a doctor, so being present during labour didn't phase me. Also, I had been told that the husband being there – a third person, aside from the doctor – helped to calm the mother.

When Rosemary went into the Nursing Home a couple of weeks before the event, my father had talked to me about the matter. He assured me that I didn't have to be present for the birth if I didn't want to. But I was of the age (28) that I wanted to share the experience with my wife and see our baby being born.

Rosemary wanted a wee girl, I said I didn't care whether it was a wee boy or a wee girl as long as the baby was healthy. But I did think that if it was a boy, I could take him to football and play cricket with him. And when I saw the baby coming out – the first thing I saw coming out was the baby's red hair! And Rosemary couldn't see from her position what I could see.

"Oh, it's a boy, it's a boy!" I declared.

Diane Weiner

War Baby

Evacuations, inoculations,
Ropes and smokes, occupations
Hide and seek, air raid shelters.
Granny's lodgers, shipyard workers,
Ration book and first bananas,
Father smuggling half Havanas.

Shell-shocked, shaky man in street,
Dragging, dragging, dragging feet.
Waste ground – wasted life
Never coming home to wife.

The Open Door

Mrs McCoy owned a little shop in the middle of our street. The street was unusual because half the houses were three storey parlour houses and the rest were kitchen houses with only two bedrooms. We considered our family a cut above those in the kitchen houses, even though my Grannie kept chickens in the backyard. The address of the parlour houses was Worchester Terrace and the kitchen houses was Chamberlain Street.

McCoys' door was always open, all and sundry tripped in from early morning to late at night. The shop was really the parlour with a counter down the middle. When I was a child it seemed so high when I was pushing my penny across it for sweets. She also sold fruit; I remember my excitement when buying my first ever banana when I was seven years old. It was 1948, after the Second World War.

The owner of the shop was a kind woman, even though she looked austere with her pinny wrapped neatly around her waist and her steel grey hair tied in a bun. She was the woman everyone turned to in times of need. She gave tick to the poor and advice to the sick. In those days, in that area, it wasn't the pub that brought people together, it was Mrs McCoy and her little shop.

Our games started and ended outside the shop: hopscotch, kick the tin, rattle the letterboxes, pirries and whips and swinging round the gas lamp-posts. I mostly remember the Neil children. There were two boys and five girls; the boys were brought up in the Protestant faith like their father and the girls were Catholic like their mother. This was commonplace and no-one thought it odd. My father was a Jew and I envied them because every one knew what a Catholic was but no one knew about the Jewish religion except what they read in the Bible. I also remember the five poor Jones children. They were often ill with T.B. and hardly ever came out to play.

One of the highlights of the year was the parades on the Twelfth of July. Irrespective of faith, we watched these parades. On the eleventh of July a huge bonfire was lit at the end of Chamberlain Street facing the Albertbridge Road. Everyone gathered round it and there was singing, dancing, and the children were given lemonade and buns; the camaraderie was shared by all. The other highlight was May Day. Every street elected their Queen to lead their parade. She had to swing on a horizontal pole and just be beautiful.

At the bottom of our street was a dance hall called the "Hut". Sometimes on summer evenings they would leave open one of the wooden doors but there was a steel grille covering the gap which we clung onto. Wide-eyed and innocent we watched the couples dance by, longing for the day when we would find a partner to call our own.

Work Experience

It was the era of the Beatles, flower power, mini skirts and free love. And yes, I do remember the sixties! For one, very good reason. I spent the summer of 1963 as a Butlin's Redcoat at Ayr in Scotland. I had never been, but my best friend had, and when the ad for the job appeared she couldn't wait to apply, and I joined her.

We went to the interview and sailed through – no wonder, we answered "yes" to every question regarding our ability to carry out all manner of duties. In the end I set out on my own. Myrtle decided to stay in her well-paid job while I left my poor family in the lurch, leaving the small shop I ran on the Shankill Road for them to look after.

The omens were good. As I boarded the little train which ran from Ayr to the camp, the driver invited me to sit up front with him. And so the experience began. There was no training given. Just one sheet telling us how to dress and how to behave: pleasant, smiling and helpful at all times. The campers helped me to survive. Many of them were seasoned guests and knew how everything worked. Once I told them I was a novice, they could not have been kinder.

My day started at 7.30am – first sitting for breakfast. There were two sittings at mealtimes, three times a day. I stood at the door, smiling and greeting all who entered. Sometimes my face was sore with smiling but I never faltered. Then there were the competitions: Holiday Princess, Glamorous Grannies, Lovely Legs, Bonnie Babies and Knobbly Knees, to name a few. I had a great laugh leading off the old-time dancing. I arranged knockout tournaments in all manner of sports. Again with absolutely no knowledge of what I was doing but with loads of enthusiasm and encouragement from others, I appeared in the Redcoat Show. As I could neither sing nor dance I ended up being the stooge for the camp comic. They even tested me for Radio Butlins, but the old Belfast accent let me down.

I was innocent and naïve when I started. I learnt what gay meant when the Entertainment Manager said he would fight me for my boyfriend, a handsome fellow who was Chief Redcoat. I got on well with my fellow workers and formed lasting friendships. It was a way to meet ordinary, decent folk and help them to enjoy their holiday.

I also learnt the true definition of hard work. We worked 16-hour days and were paid a pittance, but money could not buy the lessons of life I learnt there. It truly was the University of Life. Thank you, Mr Billy Butlin. I hope that I was able to make up for my disloyalty to my family in the years that followed. I never left them or my business again.

Diary Entry, January 1974

Sat 9th: Shop blown asunder
           "Happy New Year!"

Sun 10th: Held up at home
          By a man with a gun
          Left with a legacy
          No pills can dispel
          Forever reliving
          My weekend from Hell.

Misguided Youth

A young girl stands by my side watching my shop burn down.
"The end justifies the means," she says.
How sad, she is my employee.

The Troubles I've Seen

I've jumped over bombs
Held incendiaries in my hand
Watched a man shot dead
Had a gun to my head.

Not fighting a cause
Or taking a stance
I learnt to survive
And not be a victim.

But pity the others – so many, so many
Broken bodies, broken lives
Promises unfulfilled, dreams unrealized.

Killing with Love

She saw them everywhere, white feathers. The sign of an angel, they said, someone to watch over you. She was tempted but she never picked one up. She couldn't. Too many memories of a lesson she had learned some years before. You can kill with kindness.

It had appeared one beautiful Indian Summer day as she sat in her usual seat on the patio, enveloped in feelings of loneliness and melancholy. Memories of happier times flitted in and out of her head, That's all she had now, memories.

She knew it was no ordinary bird, it was far too beautiful. Silver and white, it's plumage a kaleidoscope of iridescent purple, pink and grey. It landed on the little stone fountain engraved with the words her mother had spoken each time she came into the garden

"God's fresh air is free"

As the bird moved ever so slowly towards her, she gently roused herself and fetched some bread which she crumbled and scattered around, making sure she left some near her chair. Sure enough, the bird came closer, showing no fear.

Soon it was waiting for her each morning. They breakfasted together. In the evenings when she returned from work it flew down to greet her. She became mesmerized by its movements and habits. She knew someone, somewhere would be searching for this lovely creature. She would try to find its owner by a message in the newspaper or radio…but not this day, not when the sun still shone and the flowers were still in bloom… when she had once again something in her life to care for and to love.

That last morning when she opened the door she was faced with a terrifying sight. The patio was a blanket of white feathers.

Friends said it was the way of nature but she knew it was her fault. She should never have fed it, never have befriended it. She should have found its owner and returned it. Because of her selfishness, the bird had become vulnerable, a prey to some predator that had come in the night and destroyed it.

Her love had killed it.

Shul

I am an outsider, yet I feel within
An affinity with this race, this creed.
I should belong, I have their blood,
Although brought up in a different world.

Unaccepted in years gone by
Surely the world has changed by now?

Yet still, I am the stranger looking in.

When you go

Leave a part of me,
            for me
The rest is yours.
Within my heart
You are still my all.

Mr Aquascutum

She had a one night stand.
Does that make her mad or bad?
It was awfully good
She was well in the mood.
He was handsome and kind
One thing on his mind.
She wanted more, but he slipped out the door.

Ships that pass in the night
Gone forever
Out of sight.

Whatever Love Is

Together forever
Or just until dawn
Two souls together
A new love is born.

Pidgin Irish

My mother's knowledge of the Irish language was limited, to say the least. She had learnt it when she was a child in Donegal where all the children were taught to speak it. I remember her saying little poems and singing songs to us when we were young. We were fascinated. Growing up in Shipyard territory, words spoken in any other tongue were unusual.

As we grew older we began to realize that my mother's Irish was different from that spoken by others. Indeed it was so unique that they could hardly recognise a word of it. Until the day we were out celebrating her seventieth birthday...

It was a lovely day and as we sat outside the restaurant enjoying the sunshine, we were joined by some friends. We discovered the wife of one of the gentlemen was also from Donegal. The wine had loosened their tongues and soon she and my mother were conversing in their very own Irish language.

It was hilarious. Neither of them had a clue what the other was saying, yet they nodded and gesticulated in unison. I have never seen such joyous expressions on the faces of two ladies talking absolute nonsense.

I treasure the memory.

Margaret Wilson

Mother's Thimble

Amongst the spools and bobbins, rainbow hued
Hidden under scissors, pins and tapes
The silver thimble lies - I pick it up
How small it is - a little tarnished now
The finger it protected, so fine-boned
Just like the lovely hand I held
While Phoebe Agnes left this world.

The Union

Everybody called it The Union. I don't know why, because it was really a workhouse and a place to be avoided at all costs.

I was there once when I was about six. Memory is a funny thing. Parts of the same event are woolly and muddled, and others so vivid that they could have occurred yesterday. The memory of my day at the workhouse is like that.

I went with my Granny to see an old neighbour of hers who was in the infirmary part of The Union. Miss McClements her name was and she had lived next door to Granny and had a lodger on whom she doted. However, I well remember the talk in my family of how he had "fleeced" Miss McClements. I didn't know exactly what that meant – the only fleece that I knew of were those on sheep. Anyway, the poor old lady who had no relatives ended up in the workhouse.

Granny was a strict, undemonstrative woman but kind-hearted nevertheless, and on learning that her old friend was ill, decided on a visit. I accompanied her because she looked after me while my mother was at work.

It must have been just after Christmas because Granny made turkey sandwiches and we never ever had turkey except at Christmas. I just vaguely remember the tram journey up the Lisburn Road and being very, very cold but said nothing, as Granny didn't like whingers.

My most vivid recollection was of the ringing noise my small shoes made on the stone floor of the infirmary and the overpowering smell of Jeyes fluid, and then to see the tiny bird-like figure in bed, clad in a scratchy, regulation nightgown. I don't know if Miss McClements ate the sandwiches. I only know that at six years of age I was terrified of this barren and heartless place. Perhaps it was aptly named after all – the union of hopelessness and helplessness that the poor creatures who ended their days there must have felt.

Fermanagh

Sweet scent of turf fire,
Lilting voices, busy hands
Smell of hens' mealy mash
Oozing through my fingers.
I rest my head on the cow's warm flank,
My hands coax creamy jets
Into the waiting bucket
While she stands patiently chewing.

My nightly visit to massive, gentle Bob;
His feathery feet move softly in the stable straw
As he nuzzles the top of my head
When he takes his apple from my hand.
Small oil lamps guide us to our beds
And blessed silence of the country night
To take our rest until the dawn,
Heralded by the rooster's raucous voice.

Lilting voices silenced now, busy hands stilled,
They sleep in consecrated ground
But yet they live – I feel them always near,
Benign and loving influence all my days.
They shaped and moulded what I am
And I shall join them in good time
And rest at peace in my heart's home,
Deep in the soft Fermanagh earth.

Cats in the Bog

John Moffitt looked tired. He had spent a long day cutting turf in his peat bog and was glad to ease himself into the comfort of his old armchair and stretch out his long legs clad in their rough, woollen work trousers, his toes in the hand-knitted socks he wore winter and summer flexing gratefully in the warmth of the turf fire. He threw a couple of sods into the back of the hearth causing a fountain of red and yellow sparks to fly upwards. The old black kettle hissed gently on the iron trivet and the nutty smell of baking bread issued from a heavy pot balanced on four embers with another four on the lid. The ancient plantation clock ticked hoarsely on the wall, gathering all its rusty wheels and mechanisms together in the ultimate effort to wheeze out the half hour.

Pushing his cap to the back of his head with a calloused finger he yawned widely and announced to no-one in particular…"Rough goin' today - that part of the bog is full of cats - nearly wrecked the loy some of them".

As a comparative newcomer to his household I said nothing, considering that it would be bad manners to ask too many questions. I was gradually coming to terms with the Fermanagh idiom my foster family used and was getting quite fond of being called "a fair wee cutty" who was jokingly admonished every day not to go chasing the "cubs" in the school playground. But ……..Cats in the Bog!!

As a ten year old who loved cats, I visualised the peat bog perhaps to be a mass graveyard for felines. I had heard awful tales about kittens being put in sacks and drowned. Was it their poor remains which were in the bog and which had almost wrecked Mr Moffitt's loy? I anxiously looked down at Daisy who was stretched out full length on my lap and silently vowed never to let her become the victim of a watery demise. I had cat-related nightmares that night but being a very curious child I asked Mr Moffitt if I could accompany him to the bog and help stack the turf. He agreed and I think was secretly pleased that I, as a town-bred child, had adapted so well to country ways. I was interested in things his two grown-up daughters had never shown an aptitude for. So we set off next morning, me steeling myself to confront the horrors of Cats in the Bog.

I was fascinated by the rhythmic wielding of the loy and how it sliced through the peat like butter, digging out with perfect symmetry the wet turfs, shining and slippery. But no cats that I could see. I kept busy helping to stack the precious fuel to dry and had almost forgotten the reason why I was there when I heard the loy strike something hard and Mr Moffitt say - "another one of those dratted cats".

Dare I look? All I could see were the geometrical cutting marks on the side of the bog; but winding serpentine through them were roots of long dead vegetation which had become petrified after lying for thousands of years in the preserving peat. These were the cats! My fears unfounded, I enjoyed the rest of my day and was extremely proud of myself when Mr Moffitt said at suppertime that the "wee town cutty" had been a big help and I never got to know why these roots were called cats.

Time

Time is nebulous – not defined by any clock
Many faceted – it can fly, drag, weigh heavily, be allotted or infinite
We can use it, waste it, or never have enough of it
Times can be ancient, modern, good or bad
Humanity is governed by time
Yet time itself is ephemeral
And we are told that on the last day time shall be no more
THEN WHAT SHALL WE DO?

Remembering Venice

City of mystery and romance – of singing gondoliers and blood
red glass,
Of whispering echoes of an ancient past
Where ghostly figures drift softly through the mists
And masked, be-jewelled courtesans, in rich and sumptuous silks
Pass with tinkling echoes of faint laughter
To keep their secret trysts with lovers.

An atmosphere of decadence pervades – the faded grandeur
crumbling
But ancient architecture still proud and dreaming
Reminder of an opulence long gone,
And still its pillars anchored in the turgid Adriatic
Which from time to time leaves high water marks
To remind Venetians that they are only there at her discretion.

Mesmeric, atmospheric – bewitching almost.
Swept back in time, I enter my own world of imagery, hand
trailing water,
The waterbus glides silently through canals and under bridges
Past the Doge's Palace still magisterial and grand.
Two bloated rubbish bags and a decomposing dog float alongside,
I retrieve my hand and am once again returned to reality.

The Accused

Inspired by a newspaper report displayed on the wall of the old Courthouse in the Ulster Folk & Transport Museum, Cultra.

The four women stood huddled together in the small cramped dock of the courthouse. Thin, undernourished and pale, none of them was more than seventeen. Eliza and Mary were sisters and held hands; Ellen and Phoebe were quietly sobbing. They were all trembling, probably from fear but also because on this bitter January morning there was no heat of any kind in the austere courtroom.

The place was packed with offenders, police and a couple of solicitors all awaiting the arrival of the Resident Magistrate. The buzz of conversation died when a large florid man in a tweed suit appeared and took his seat on the raised chair beside the dock. This was the man who would dispense his own brand of justice to the four women.

The clerk read the list of offences. They had been caught by the night watchman pilfering coal in Mr Arbuthnot's coal yard. They had gained access through a broken fence and filled an old hessian sack with coal which was piled ready for delivery to the local mill. The value of coal in the sack had been estimated to be worth four shillings.

Justice meted out was swift without any form of appeal from the hapless women. They would each have to pay 2/6d. - a half-crown; failure to do so would result in them being sent to a reformatory.

It was paid.

Eliza pawned two thin blankets from her bed, her mother's wedding ring and Mary's only pair of boots. Ellen and Phoebe did not have anything to pawn, so they sold themselves. "Justice" was served.

Now I'm Eighty

Old Age is not for sissies, I've heard somebody say
And I would like to second that and point out, if I may
That though we hear of pensioners who go off bungee jumping
We never see them having CPR and cardiac thumping.
They say we're living longer and I'm sure that it's true,
But how's it done and is it good... I think I've got the clue:
We've pills for this and jabs for that – we've zimmers by the score.
Our GPs sit with pencil poised and ask, "You need some more?"
We've hearing aids and plastic hips and spare part bits and bobs,
We've even teeth transplanted into gummy gobs.
Our surgeries are full of old folk needing medication
Who cling to life no matter what with utmost dedication.
So often frail old bodies outlive a failing brain
For which there is no remedy although they search in vain.
In days gone by pneumonia was then "The Old Man's Friend";
No drugs prescribed, no treatment given – a really peaceful end.
But now we're treated, jabbed and drugged by people we don't know.
They "counsel" us and tell us that we mustn't feel so low,
They call us "dear" and speak quite loud, enunciating clearly,
They patronise and try to sound as though speaking sincerely.
As for myself I'd just hate that and hope my end is quick,
I'd love to go out smiling – no pain and never sick.
We cannot choose what way we'll go, but if I'm really ill,
I don't want to be resussed by any magic pill;
My Living Will will clearly state in letters big and bold:
SHE CHOSE TO OPT FOR DNR ...so now you have been told!!

Winter 2010

I remember, I remember – it started last December
The snow and ice descended – and we were quite offended
"It's far too early," we all cried – "We like our Christmases more mild."
We slithered and we slipped… some even fractured hips
The pavements were like glass… the roads like Glenshane Pass
Clearing same: AGAINST THE LAW – so we prayed fervently for thaw
Water flowed and gushed unheeded – but what we really, really needed
Was a little for our tea – and to flush when we went to wee.
We queued for hours for our supplies… but it came as no surprise
The water service: NOT TO BLAME – the local councils:
                    MUCH THE SAME
After all, who would have guessed – snow in winter? I fear you jest!
Come this December, hibernate – either that or emigrate!

With Apologies to Holman Hunt

The door did not have a key, a keyhole or even a handle. It looked impenetrable – solid, heavy, uncompromising. I would never know what was on the other side.

I was wrong. One day it swung silently and easily open. Sunshine flooded over me and there was a winding pathway on the other side. I stepped through and have never regretted it. The path was not always even and sometimes the terrain was rough. But I had a strong hand to hold and a smile to encourage me. And they both belonged to Fred.

Biographical notes

Jim Bradley
Was born in East Belfast and has spent most of his life in the city. Attended several schools, as the family moved house quite a bit. Worked as a shoe salesman, then in a large bakery, and finally in the health service, before retiring early. Started writing through the Engage With Age project and has been writing ever since.

John Galbraith
A retired Civil Servant living in East Belfast. In 2001 joined a B.I.F.H.E. (now the Belfast Met.) Creative Writing class tutored by Ruth Carr and has been writing ever since. Some poems published in *The Lonely Poet's Guide to Belfast* and further Poetry in Motion anthologies. Founder member of *Words Alive*.

Myra Gibson
Sang for years in The Performers' Club under the direction of Mr Frank Capper. Has penned a few poems in her time, and quite a few more since joining *Words Alive* writing group in Ballyhackamore Library. Has also enjoyed meeting and making new friends. Published in Poetry in Motion anthologies, *New Belfast* and *Write Up There* (New Belfast Community Arts Initiative) and in *A Sense of Place* (United Press).

Kate Glackin

A retired secretary and avid reader. Joined the class to express her thoughts and ideas. Enjoys weekly walking group, R.S.P.B. outings, charitable work, the Speakers' Circle and regularly attends the theatre and concerts of the Ulster Orchestra.

Gladys Hull

Born in Newry, 1948. Wife and home-maker, interested in creative writing, arts and crafts, and indoor bowling. Loves to travel and observe this wonderful world. Has gained several awards from Belfast Metropolitan College.

David G Hull

Spent time in Africa, now based in Belfast and engaged in creative writing. Interests include watercolour painting, music and dry-stone-walling. Has published several booklets. Currently working on a biography of his parents.

Denis Hyde

A retired warehouse worker with a hearing problem since birth, but still engaged in many interests. These include reading, bowls and films. Got involved with creative writing since retiring.

Joan Lawlor

A piano teacher for many years (in fact, she taught George Smythe many moons ago!) As a widow she turned to writing to express her grief through poetry. A founder member, Joan gave the writing group its name, *Words Alive*.

Jim McClean

A retired aircraft engineer who was a member of the design team at Shorts. Cajoled into joining *Words Alive* at its embryonic stage and helped set it on a secure footing. Departed this life Christmas 2010 and is fondly remembered and sorely missed.

Sue McCrory

A widow, mother and grandmother. Started writing by accident, after attending a *Words Alive* open day event in the library. Delighted to become one of the group, to learn from everyone, hearing their stories and to begin writing her own.

John Mc Guckin

A crusader of personal, political and social truths. Used to go to the bricklaying in the mornings, then slip upstairs and write a poem. It was a hobby never disclosed. Now, with two books self-published, it's more than a hobby, a way of life.

Marie Mathews

D.o.b. 10th April, 1936. Retired civil servant, "unclaimed treasure". Interests include writing, politics, the theatre and travel; also meeting others through older people's organisations; on a voluntary basis trying to make life better for the vulnerable in our society; and wining and dining whenever possible! Founder member of *Words Alive.*

George Smythe

Born in 1924. Worked as a rep selling Olivetti typewriters all over Northern Ireland. Has one son, three daughters, ten grandchildren, and one great grandson. A member of the Philharmonic Chorus for 33 years, he never missed a Messiah! Founder member of *Words Alive* with many stories to tell.

Diane Weiner

A semi-retired business woman. Inspired to put pen to paper to capture childhood memories. Joined the class one year ago and has been encouraged by the support and generosity of fellow members.

Margaret Wilson

A retired secretary, wife, mother and grandmother. Likes music, theatre and other people's poetry. Formerly a member of a B.I.F.H.E. (now the Belfast Met.) Creative Writing Group and has been published in *Poetry Now, Masters of Humorous Verse* and Poetry in Motion Anthologies, and was a winner of Downtown Radio's Short Story Competition and Relate's *Recipe for a Happy Family*.